At the Edge
Wrth yr Ochr

© Stuart Elliott 2024

Artwork © Chloe Elliott

All Rights Reserved

Published by

Independent Publishing Network

To those we love

There are no words to say the sorrow

that broken hearts breaking mend.

No cry to reach the depths deserved

of desolations voice, save the stillness

of another's calm embrace to hold

the love flown down in falling tears.

22nd July 2024

In fond memory of Helen, with love to John.

To those we have loved and let go. To those who have inspired these words. To Helen, Becca, Chloe and Arwel: The Cat, you're all in here somewhere.

With grateful thanks to Ruth Fabby MBE for her expert guidance and editing.

Contents

To those we love	5
Forward: at the Edge	11
On Pilgrimage	14
Coffin Trail	15
Pilgrim Friend	16
The Cake	17
Ffynnon Mair	18
The Green Man	19
Seiriol - Enlli	20
Solstice Pilgrims	21
Walk on	22
Meadow	24
Unfolding the Heavens	25
The Gift	26
Gather	27
Encounters	28
Gathering Hope	29
Coda	30
Crumbs	31
Olives and Bread	32
Bread Broken	33
Women of the Passion	34

Anointed	35
Questioning	36
Weeping	37
Witness	38
Enduring	39
Preparing	39
Dawning	40
Revelation	40
Revolution	40
A Word for the Flesh	42
Just the Shoes	44
For Kaz	46
Did We Miss You	47
In Nature	48
Angel Moth	49
Moth	50
Epiphany	51
A Little Something	52
Waters Meet	53
Lost in the Flow	54
A Part or Apart	55
Words	56
Candlemas Bells	57

In the Crowd	58
Strands of Fragility	59
Gweld Y Gwir trwy'r Gwyll	60
Nations Divide	62
Capel Nant	63
Tymhorau	64
Seasons	65
Earthed	68
On Grief	70
Grief	71
Blossom	72
Fox	73
Church Closed	74
Seeds	75
Autumn Sun	76
Empty Vase	77
Space Between the Trees	78
Eternity	80
What Is Gone	81
Creation	82
Chaos	83
Re-Creation	84
Autumn Saint Autumn Sun	85

Morning Prayer	86
The Cat	87
In Memoriam - a Last Pair of Shoes	90

Forward: at the Edge

In nature the edge is abundant with life It is diverse and multilayered yet complex and often messy. The edge of a forest has many more species of plants than the centre. A lane hedgerow is all edge and often abundant with wild flowers and grasses.

Where Sea meets Shore, where Horizon meets Sky, where Land meets Water, where a Path meets the Grassy Verge and where we too encounter the other. Permaculture is the human attempt to create more edge in agriculture or a garden. The Edge is also the meeting place for the human.

These poems are of the edge, of encounters. Waves crash on a shore and the beach pebbles are rearranged. For a moment something new is revealed. The challenge is to capture it. Words come in those moments when emotions surface touching deep in the soul. The poems write themselves. I am the scribe giving voice to that which often has no spoken voice of its own.

There are four themes at the edge: Pilgrimage, People, Nature and encounters with Grief.

These are all edge places. Going out on pilgrimage is an intentional stepping out of the everyday. It brings us into contact with others. Conversation is somehow easier whilst walking and sharing the road together.

The people in these poems are at the edge of society. They are on the fringe, those overlooked or passed by. Some of these people we find images of in biblical narratives. We find these characters and events replayed in our modern daily life.

The connections to nature attempt to give words to something which already has a voice of its own. These poems give a narrative of encounters, the conversations, between rest of nature and the human.

Grief. I was most surprised to find so many poems about grief and death, what we often call 'loss'.

Whist the death of someone close is a 'loss' they are not lost. For once, we know exactly where they are! The important task of grief is to pay attention to moving from a life with to a life without. When this task is neglected, grief becomes more difficult, broken. This is reflected in the poem 'What is gone' which changed after a conversation (you'll see when you get to it), the last line is as you said it should be. I wrote it differently, but was wrong. Thank you.

If there is an enduring image in the biblical narrative about being at the edge, it is the 'Hem of the Garment'.

There is an undercurrent of a spiritual theme which relates to this biblical image of the edge of the cloak of Jesus. In desperation a woman reaches for the hem of Jesus' robe believing he can make her well. It is a story made all the more important when Jesus then enters the house of a senior official from the temple - one who would have been complicit in the exclusion of the very woman who had just come into contact with Jesus.

If, as theology suggests, the people of church are the body of Christ, the outer garment of church is those places of encounter, then the hem of the garment is the most important place.

It is the place to which those who have been excluded elsewhere might also find 'A Touching Place'. This hymn by John Bell and Graham Maule, intended for a service of healing, suggests the task is worthy of our time and effort. The task then is to intentionally dwell in, create and sustain these edge places.

On Pilgrimage

Coffin Trail

An out of the way place offers a moment
to rest; on the way, though the path is not
easy up the winding trail the coffins went
once horse-drawn over part river bed.
It offers no sleep for those weary of life.

As the bell tolls drawing us on,
the walls enclose, comfort,
become as an old friend.
Sacred and secular are drawn here
not for hymns or liturgies.
But, for an ancient simple silence offered
by wood and stone. Walkers intent on their
journey become pilgrims for a time and stop
awhile to refresh in the generous welcome.

The mountain and path beyond calls for those
who would seek out its solitude for their soul.
As quietness returns,
the walls and stone
await new visitors,
to bathe in an experience of the other.

Pilgrim Friend

There is a connection of unspoken conversation
which drifts between worlds when walking.
Journeying together.
We become more than two souls on a road.
That spirit expands again at journey's end.
We who remain are hungry
for more than bread broken.
Then, the space between us has changed,
and though we part we are as close as before,
as if we never left the path.
Until the next time my pilgrim friend.

The Cake

There was a pause before the cake
was announced, and a smile because,

(not that there was very much doubt
it was inevitable really that we would
celebrate her birthday with Victoria sponge
buttercream and raspberry jam.)

because,
It was not her favourite,
But his.

Ffynnon Mair

Ffynnon Mair
is not hidden
from view, but
facing Enlli.
Yet a visitor must
approach her down a
rugged cliff edge not made
for humans trespassing by.
No casual tourist turns up here
for a sympathetic blessing.
This is a hard place
appropriate for Mary.
The sea is caught on the rocks,
thrown up in sunlight, refracted
droplets held for a moment before us,
like memories, we see a glimpse of them before
they return. Each new wave a fragment of the path
that brought us to her in-between place.
Neither land nor sea, rock face nor shore line
salt nor fresh. We cannot stay long, for this
is neither the end of our journey
nor yet, the beginning of the next.

The Green Man

The Green Man,
with the weight of the world
upon his bearded face.
Sleeps.
Unborn.
Awaiting the moment
to arise from her salt fresh womb
and we await his coming
to reconcile and heal the earth.

A serendipitous image of Ffynnon Mair, Uwchmynydd, Pen Llyn with the Green Man awaiting rebirth.

Seiriol - Enlli

Sat in Seiriol's sight what would such a saint
make of us waiting for the tide? Earth rolls
toward the light which dawns around
as oceans, quiet now roll gently by.

Enlli, in memory only, as elusive as the silken light
which slips through the clouds of the morning.

Perhaps we were neither ready
nor worthy to visit her shore this time;
to wait among the stones,
to listen for distant echoes.

Until we cast off the burdens of our need
and sow within ourselves the way of providence.
Her draw continues to encourage our yearning that
one day as we come to who we are,
we might just be fit and ready for the kingdom.

Realising then almost too late,
it has been with us all the way.

Solstice Pilgrims

As the light fades on this shortest of days

May we who have walked to the turn of the earth

dwell as companions of brightness.

With winter's shrouded colours born of waiting

in anticipation of the light to come.

May we return to this moment when the darkness

closes in and be cradled as in candlelight

encouraged as by bird song,

a haunting vespers which invades

our inner silence and calls companions

and friends together out towards the light.

Walk on

Take off your shoes and walk a mile in mine
Walk in step unknowing beside companions
Walk slowly alongside those we nurture
Walk with an offer of hospitality and
  sanctuary to those we meet.

Walk with the inspiration to take a lighter journey
Walk with joy in every season
Walk on a wide path with those we meet rarely
Walk on to catch but a glimpse of those far off
Walk with kindred spirits from other islands
Walk with souls connected at the deep down

Walk on with a shared past,
  a story of struggle or pain
Walk offering gifts, or generous words
Walk with a conversation
  picked up from the last journey
Walk with poets whose words will weave our path.

Walk with a protest on our lips
  and a banner in our heart
Walk with those who hold us in prayer
and with those for whom we must pray

Walk with those who offer a new challenge
Walk close to those who are a challenge
Walk softly with those who find us the same.

Walk with a shared chance encounter
Walk, lives connected, weaving in and out
Walk with those who sing
Walk gently with those we wish would not sing.

Walk as artists gathering the colours of nature
Walk with those we have carried
  and allow them to carry us in their turn

Walk with the gentle ones,
  and those who could learn to be gentle
Walk with a vision to go further than we can go
Walk a woven path with the friends
of friends of friends.

Walk with those who make us laugh at ourselves
Walk with those whose words will carry us until our
  walking days are done
Walk in the company of strangers who
at journey's end become friends.

Meadow

The meadow where the orchids lay

gone now to seed, is silent save

for the river dancing over stones,

the chitter of some birds unknown,

And the ghosts of pilgrims lying here

in the grass as conversations drift

back like old friends to a party long

Gone, but not quite finished.

Unfolding the Heavens

I can do no more than stand in wonder whilst earth rises to each footfall. Silken skies crowned in hues of light bright lit for the moment.

Haloed, darkening
as the remains of the day's sun
and rising moon co create the eternal.

I might have disbelieved myself had we not walked in company. For the gift was composed by our time together; in the limited liminal hours our memories Now painted with the brightness
of the unfolding heavens.
A dream of time, stood still, to dwell;

The Gift

I imagine you

walking the opposite way

arriving at the marker post from

the other direction. Disappearing

into tussocks, sunk deep into the sodden

landscape. Swallowed up or sucked down.

Visible for a brief moment then gone.

Like signposts in life.

As flashes of brightness that leave an image

greying into the mists of memory.

Thoughts cloud and change
what was once clear and sharp.

Your way ahead the path I've walked

Is your past, mine for the future.

Our gift to each other.

Gather

Storm clouds gather on the edge.

We step out of the mould into generous arms.

Yearning for experiences in the rain and the sun.

At the edge, distant dreams of longing, to be on the journey. Where fun and laughter are encouraged.

Hospitable, playful colours and flavours.

Laugh and dance like the Winds.

Gathered, to be sent;

Encounters

Gathering Hope

Influence and honesty
testimony of austerity
traditional melodies; a
collection for the soul.

Gathering spontaneity
eclectic, and evolving
heartfelt lyrical music,
reflection and prayer.

God in creativity
breathing humanity
activist imperfection
protesting injustice,
seeking asylum.

Gathering passion
travelling inspiring,
journey with justice
sustaining and liberating
melodies of communities,
poetic reflections to
Lament, Hope and Inspire.

Coda

The gentle imperative that begins
deep in your heart. The whisper that
will not let go no matter how hard
you try to ignore it. As the beating
drum of the world, goes on insisting
the path we tread. Turn aside, see
before us the waters are stirred up.
There is an agitation that will not give,
until, we rise, in answer to the cry.
To catch the moment. That brings to
birth in us a new beginning.

Coda. Cymraeg – the imperative to rise up – or in Beibl.net Proverbs 31.9 'Coda dy lais' – Speak out, raise your voice.

Coda. Music – the piece of music at the end which reflects on all that has been before, yet remains independent.

Crumbs

Our table is covered in crumbs.
I feel your disapproval growing.
An unwelcome guest in our midst.
There are none such at this table.
Even the disapproving are welcome too.
Gather the crumbs. Not untidy but loved.
Much bread has been broken around it.

Broken and shared this bread
  will sustain our journey.
Crumbs fall, a story of those left behind.
Blessed be God
In the scattered crumbs that forever remain,
As precious as those shared and eaten.

Olives and Bread

Olives and Bread.

Everlasting old. New creation.

Grown. Baked.

Plucked from a tree. Crafted by hands.

In the maturing. Worked and proven.

For a Bitter Sweet moment of life together

Of grace. Christ and Earth cannot

belong together for long.

Bread Broken

A fractured loaf
the crust breaks
crumbs fall and
the heart is exposed.
In the tearing apart
strands cling together
like sinews,
then suddenly opening up
the heart of the loaf.

Whole, it is of little use. Broken,
It becomes the Bread of Life.
Breaking bread is wholeness preluded.

Women of the Passion

Anointed

You risked it all.

In a moment of emotion

charged with an energy

that heightened the senses

as perfumed hands, feet, and hair,

mingled for a time.

Physical touch, in kindness, sorrow and love.

Knowing somehow

another chance would not come.

Mary took a pound of costly perfume made of pure nard, anointed Jesus' feet, and wiped them with her hair. The house was filled with the fragrance of the perfume. John 12:3

Questioning

Hidden in the half light and shadows,

were you desperately seeking the truth

with a piercing gaze over firelight?

The courage to speak out

was rewarded with a betrayal of the truth.

Then a servant-girl, seeing him in the firelight, stared at him and said, "This man also was with him." Luke 22:56

Weeping

Anguished tears flow

for a moment passing by

for the loss, pain and

a fear that grips

like cords tightening

deep in the soul

longing for another turning.

"Daughters of Jerusalem, do not weep for me, but weep for yourselves and for your children." Luke 23:28

Witness

Huddled together

against the jeering

and mocking of the condemned,

distant but engaged still.

You who once sustained

now resigned,

not powerless but waiting,

where others deserted,

the faithful remnant.

There were also women looking on from a distance; among them were Mary Magdalene, and Mary the mother of James the younger and of Joses, and Salome.

Mark 15:40

Enduring

You, there at the beginning, now at the ending. The sword of sorrow promised for your heart has pierced your soul. In silent loyal vigil receiving a taste of the bitter cup.

With gritted teeth 'according to your word' comfort to another's son.

"Woman, here is your son." John 19:26

Preparing

Still you follow, unwavering. Quietly you defy authority watching, waiting for the right moment, for swords have no power here. Your peaceful action, begins the silent revolution-echo through the centuries. Keep watch.

The women who had come with him from Galilee followed, and they saw the tomb and how his body was laid. Luke 23:55

Dawning

You return expectant, of nothing more than the task of loving service to anoint the departed. You who have been there through it all, now in the final moment as the earth turns to the sun in the quietness of the morning after.

Suddenly unprepared

Revelation

for the moment you found everything changed confused in disarray both hearts and tomb lay empty before you no place to lay flowers or memorial. What then now but to flee away until, until before you,

not stone,

but word softly spoken

Revolution

calling you by name with tears of sadness and joy unburdened now of your first telling the emotions ride out. Nervous whispers permeate gatherings of those who misunderstood for now it begins.

And very early on the first day of the week, when the sun had risen, they went to the tomb. Mark 16:2

So they went out and fled from the tomb, for terror and amazement had seized them; and they said nothing to anyone, for they were afraid. Mark 16:8

Now it was Mary Magdalene, Joanna, Mary the mother of James, and the other women with them who told this to the apostles. Luke 24:10

A Word for the Flesh

The Word became Wisdom and lived among us.
But foolishly we missed its simplicity.
So the Word became Light and lived among us,
But we smothered its flame.
Then Word became Truth and lived among us,
But we disbelieved its sincerity.
And the Word became Hope and lived among us,
But we scorned its optimism.
So the Word became Patience and lived among us,
But we chased it away in our anxiety.
Then the Word became Peace and lived among us,
But we trampled on its careful footsteps.
And the Word became Strength among us
But we were caught out in our weakness.
So the Word became Understanding among us
But we misunderstood in our haste to know.
Then the Word became Kindness among us
But we exploited its openness.
When the Word became Generosity among us
We abused its hospitality.
So the Word became Self control among us
but we mocked its prudence.

Then the Word became Goodness,
Though we were lost in complacency.
And the Word became Humility,
But we were puffed up on our own ego.
So the Word became Gentleness,
But we refused to be tender.
And when the Word became Love,
We rejected it in anger.

So the Word became Flesh full of Wisdom, Light and Truth, Hope, Patience and Peace. Strength, Understanding and Kindness. Generosity, Self control and Humility. Goodness, Gentleness and Love. And lived among us.

And; Cradled in its warmth, welcoming its insight, captivated by its brightness, Revelling in its honesty, Engaged with its vision, Waiting with diligence, Dwelling within its boundaries. Supported in its embrace, Cherishing its knowledge, Partnered in its friendship, Gifted with abundance, Recognising our abandon, Humbled by its letting go, Receiving its mercy and, Held in its compassion:
We might, at last, glimpse its glory.

Just the Shoes

                        Was it you that day?
                   I forgot to ask your name.
            On the steps – you fell
        backwards, I turned
    too late.

You, crumpled,

cracked, your head at my feet.

We wait together on the steps for
  help to come, head cradled now in my lap
    crying out for your shoe. It came off, I guess.

I don't recall, like your name, when you fell.

'Don't worry about your shoes, you need to be still'

I said.

They came.

'What's your name?'

They asked.

You went in the ambulance with both your shoes.

Why those shoes?

As I walked away through the crowd.

Perhaps fashionable, expensive.

I don't know.
Ordinary trainers to me, a little scuffed
around the edges, like the rest of you. I realise,
scuffed around the edges is what people see,
the names they call you, what does it matter
when, if you reply or not
it's always the same meaning
'not here',

'move on',

'don't be in my way,'

When was it that we saw you?

But your shoes. The only pair you had.
No name to me just the shoes
because you needed them.

Funny. How I remember
the shoes, but not your name.

For Kaz

You offered me a smile when I stopped to speak.
I guess it was all you had to give away.
But I will carry your smile with me
and hold it close.

You were wrapped in your duvet and woolly hat
clutching a small handful of change.
I was wrapped in my concern for direction clutching
a device designed to connect.

You asked me for nothing.

In those precious minutes our worlds' collide.
You will have forgotten my face in the crowd
that passes you by.
But I will carry your smile with me and hold it close.

For I dared to turn aside from
the world across the street with
the well heeled whose eyes don't
meet yours or break their focussed concern.

Amidst it all:
I heard your cry. 'Scuse me?'
And your gift, a simple smile
carries me on, lightens my heart.

I met Kaz on a street corner in Cardiff City Centre.

Did We Miss You

You arrived late.
You always did
as I recall and,
you came and sat there
in the midst of them. One
or two moved up to give you space
in the crowded room though that
might have been on account of your
eclectic clothing and unkempt hair.

Yet, your bright eyes and half smile
spoke a thousand different stories.

The great and the good were there
and the speaker offered profound words
into the gathering of responsibility and
representation.

Did we fulfil them in our welcome?
Or, once again, miss you sitting
amongst us, waiting for an invitation.

For Ifor who was always there, and often ignored.

In Nature

Angel Moth

The angel moth sits in my path
hopping from grass blade to grass blade,
then as I stop for a time she lands on my glove.

Wings of such delicate near white splendour
and skeletal beauty,
barely it seems,
enough to hold her in the air yet,
she flits with ease between grasses when
she chooses, now, to sit on my hand.

An angel visited me and stayed for a while and I
was captivated by her presence
and unfathomable beauty.

Moth

You could have been mistaken for lichen had I not noticed your buff dusty green silken wings.

So captivated in an awkward moment, I clung to a ladder at the top of a wall.

My efforts clumsy compared to yours sat quietly, nothing, holding you to the lime mortar.

I am the fragile one who will break if I fall, you are strength and beauty before me.

I challenge paint suppliers to represent the complexity of your shade in name or hue.

You are to me, for a moment, all that there is.

As I retreat, return to work, my gaze continues to be drawn to your perch high on the wall.

Unmoved still.

Epiphany

A light and a fear.

High above the gloom of a valley
shrouded in the orange glow of neon
a misty halo surrounds an old light.
Captivating, white, with its bright against
black, skies no others dare invade.
Light enough for now. To lead.

She rises over the distant hill.
Drawing the wonder:
Is it brighter on the other side?

The chasm gapes
as she moves step by step
and we, roll, ever eastward
her path different.

Later.

Stars return to their place
so many, more than before.
She has gone her way
and I missed the chance to follow, yet
like the skies that night, I am brighter.
I carry her with me.

A Little Something

Our world seems weary of its winter coat.

Clouds part, and blue lies beyond.

A soft blue streaked with white cotton

as if nothing was ever happening beneath.

It is gone almost as soon as it arrived,

Perhaps I was not supposed to see it.

A change of scene, a glimpse backstage.

Though I wonder as clouds are drawn

and the sky reveals a little of herself:

If only I could live in that short moment and

could treat each encounter as such a gift?

Waters Meet

A foot in each river is mirror to my soul
 but minor disturbance to the ever onward flow.

Like the way the waters meet and run together.

How the edges turn gently pooling.

Where eddies still rippled lose focus.

As dappled surface renders depths unknown.

When grey rocks colour underwater.

There is no carrying these things
 which make heavy burdens light.

Water cupped into hands is river no more.

Memories of beauty contained undivided let go

And become her unrelenting stream
 of energy and ever onward flow.

Lost in the Flow

I am lost in the flow

I am tumbled over

I am rippled with swirling beauty

I am content, at peace inspired

I am the tranquil sussurus

Until at breaking point unknown

I am overpowered in the unending undertow

I am waterfalling,
sparkling, translucence overflowing,
until, crushed, thrown, the sky refracted.

I am intricately woven again and lost in the flow.

A Part or Apart

Reaching out to touch a tree

Standing in the shadow of branches

Swimming between rocks

Catching the light of the sun upon my face

Apart from, or, a part of this?

Drawn to touch the mirror glass surface

Suddenly shattered, a thousand shards reflect back

The light and yet

Withdraw and it recomposes.

One touch rippled outwards for an age

waves of disturbance radiate away

as if something unwanted.

A gentler touch, the water parts, allows space
within; To participate alongside,

caressing sunlight reflected

The potential of all things cradled
in the palm of my hand.
I must immerse myself to be a part.

Words

On returning. The chapel has
  become a place of so many words.
Eyelids are weighted down but
Blessed Sleep ought not come here
Understanding is far from me
Muted understanding
Like underwater trying to
  listen to the conversation above.
And I'm drowning in the torrent
Of worthy advice.
Oh for the hills of yesterday.

Candlemas Bells

If there were a flower for prophecy it would be the snow-white bells arriving early in time for Candlemas. Arrogant even, a brash flower, cutting through the cold earth it comes resilient, hardy. Beauty beguiles their strength.
Amidst the darkness expectant of the warmth to come, our instinct is to light candles. An incandescent dream. Inefficient of light but life enough to stir the soul into speaking. The snowdrop, harbinger of those who hear the silent call to defiance of convention.

In the Crowd

There in the crowd.

A half smile, world weary but

with gestures of warmth.

There again.

soft words a voice of

understanding amidst pain.

A slow pace.

walking with empathy

alongside broken hearts

and damaged lives.

Vulnerable, humble.

Unarmed.

Strands of Fragility

Darkness hangs upon us
so much broken
strands of fragility
a peace we once knew
now forgotten.

A different place a different time
the cruelty we still cannot comprehend
violence that ought not be possible in
our world and yet the veil is drawn.
Comments from critics pick the carcass
bones of the latest happening.

Then one small act
not random, probably selfish
but a kindness in the midst of the darkness.
And a light flickers.
A light of hope born
out of desperation. A fragile love
cradled with desire,
to see it grow,
to see it shared.

Gweld Y Gwir trwy'r Gwyll

See the truth through the half-light

An 8' by 16' mural painted by Chloe during lockdown to cover the front of our extension whilst the wall had been removed. Parts of this are now embedded in the building.

A dark fear grips. Masks of
pain and suffering hidden
from view distanced.

Thin cloth, veils, separates.
Barely visible, breath
becomes lost confidence
in setting out emerging
unfolding unraveling
the tangle of tied up lock
downs within ourselves to
undo the stepping back
withdrawing of past hurts.

Time to heal, forgive,
allow the letting go, unfurl
in a tentative stretch
out toward the other.

To learn again a gentle touch.

Nations Divide

Walking a lake shore
as nations divide
a place apart on the edge
of something new.

Amidst the darkness
expectations arise of the light
that touches hearts with
kindnesses the world forgot.

Alongside ordinary folk
simple words
honest hands
changing lives.

In the face of confrontation
withdraw
gather
and heal.

Capel Nant

We stand and watch
what remains of an orange-red glow
Slips gently through a gap between sea and clouds
Past the edge of the sea
as clouds shift to change its final form.

Our eyes cannot hold its gaze for long.
The infectious silence breaks
and with a sigh the last ember winks out:
Which betrays our knowing
that the sun will rise no more to our cry,
Than God Will Change,
for our latest whim.

Earth turns in the light
and we who stand see the beauty no more.

So we too must turn and be warmed
by the light that continues on.
To wait, and to see once again
of the beauty and brightness
that once delighted us.

Nant Gwyrtheyrn is a former quarry village. Now a Welsh language centre. The Chapel balcony looks northwest over the sea.

Tymhorau

Calan Gaeaf

Cysgir natur, daw'r tywyllwch
Rhwng bywydau daearol a dragwyddol
Tenau'r fêl gwawn

Alban Arthan

Cynhelir mewn golau cannwyll
Calonogir gan drydar
Disgwylir y golau gwawrio

Gwanwyn Celtaidd

Gwydn ond gostyngedig gyda'u
pen i lawr yn erbyn y gaeaf gwyllt.
Fel bydwragedd canant hwy:
'Mae e gerllaw'

Alban Eilir

Arhoswch a gwyliwch y gad llonydd
daearu troi heibio am orffwys.
cymododd trwy farwolaeth aileni

Seasons

All Hallows

Nature sleeps, the dark comes
Between temporal and eternal worlds
The veil thins to gossamer.

Winter Solstice

Cradled in candlelight
Encouraged by birdsong
Anticipating the light to come

Celtic Spring

Determined but humble with
heads hung low against the wild winter.
As midwife they sing: 'It is at hand'

Spring Equinox

Watch and wait the letting go

earthed laid out to rest

reconciled through death, reborn

Geni'r Haf

O'r Hendref i'r Hafod.

Preswylir o'r Gaeaf i'r Haf.

Ymestyn, dysgu llawenhau.

Alban Hefin

Coda, distewi, synfyfyrio

yng nghanol yr haf dros yr olygfa

ymlaen ac yn ôl cyn disgynnol

Gŵyl Awst

Ymgasglu o gwmpas tân

Gwilio bara tyfu a coginio

Straeon bara am heddiw

Alban Elfed

Cywain cynhaeaf ynghyd

a cwrdd mewn

cysgodfa enaid ei gilydd

Birth of Summer

From the Hearth onto the heath.

Winter to summer dwelling.

Stretching, learning to rejoice.

Summer Solstice

Rise up, becalm, contemplate

at midsummer the view ahead

behind before descending

Lammas

Gathered around a fire

Watching bread rise and cook

Stories of bread for today

Autumn Equinox

Gathering the harvest together

and meeting within

the shelter of each other's soul

Earthed

If we had but a glimpse of the world
as a resting place would we be caught
in the sacred story? Honoured as the
whole of life becomes a day of preparation.
We might just then become co-creators
of the dawn for a divine re-imagining of
the lost art and beauty of creation. A life laid
fallow, for a time, is not in vain. To let go,
to allow the natural restfulness to rise up
and with gentle ease, to participate;
earthed once again.

On Grief

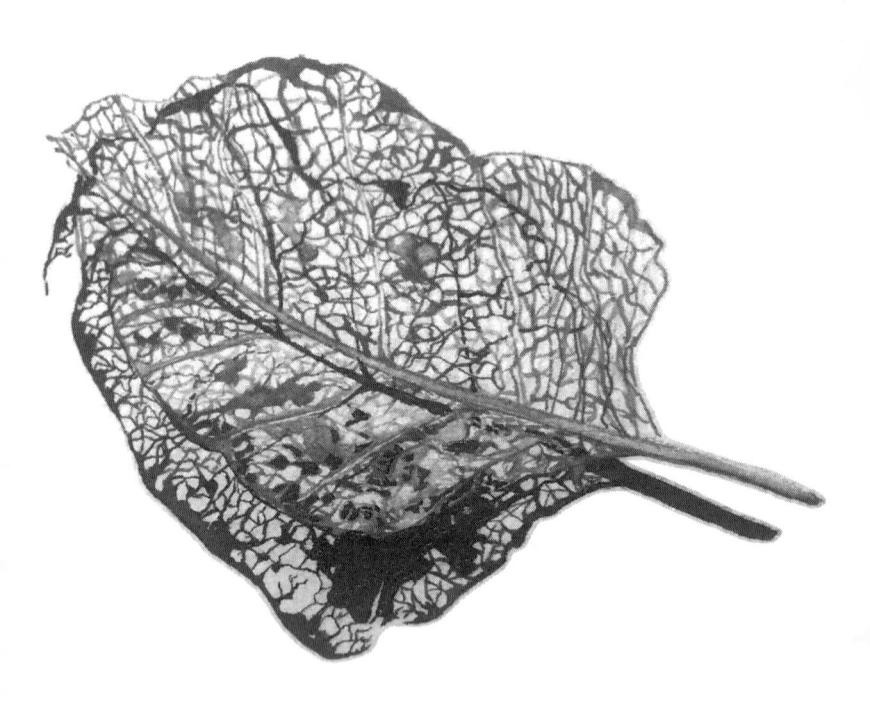

Grief

I have seen a glimpse of a place not yet,
covered as if with glistening dew
  in the morning sun,
being prepared for me to dwell in.

I am not there yet. I am but a sapling learning how to grow in a new clearing when a tree falls.

Emptiness, around, beckons like an early sun's lighting of a summer cloud above the morning mist.

Serene, with promise. That which fell as harsh rain might yet fall sweet. Refreshing, drawing me onwards, encouraging growth.

Blossom

We go from the graveyard. It is

enveloped in silence once again.

On our way, the trees blossom with birdsong

filtering down to the hoard

of black clad mourners walking by.

Effortless melody humbles

the feeble tunes we sang.

Our discordant attempt to speak of

the unseen in that liminal space is

lacking. The bird's song

a rite both spiritual and elemental.

Fox

The fields were full of the sound of the kids, young, days old if that, dancing and singing their way along the path, except they were not. They knew before me the fox was there. I saw him slide away into the gorse a chance sly glance over the shoulder reveals that diners to a late lunch have been interrupted but he has a takeaway. He runs low in a wide circle returning to the table. The goats and their kids gather to mourn.

Church Closed

Church Closed. Graveyard Open.

Are only the dead welcome now?

Standing in the quiet hills life around

begins to emerge, or perhaps I being still

of heart become aware of its presence.

Amongst the flourishing grasses unknown

wild flower seeds have come and put down

their roots over which the occasional visitor treads.

The walls of grey stone sit silently here.

Songs once from within at an end.

Yet here outwith the walls there is a

full chorus as life takes back this ancient

space. And worship begins, as we let it grow

within a heart that sings once again

of love and beauty.

Wild, untamed, open and free.

Seeds

Have you seen the seed selection?
Packets with pictures of prize
winning marrows and flowers
in bloom. Like a thousand prisoners
those seeds hang on death rows
awaiting release. Sow by date
stamped on each packet. A life
sentence without parole. Starving
inside foil for freshness, the irony
a seed is fresh when born.

I too have held them prisoner,
captive since last summer, in a
jar among the spices and packets
of unknown contents on a shelf.

Poppy seeds with potential to
grow into golden patches of sunlight
pushing up anywhere they might fall.

For Ann who shared her poppy seeds with me. Pabi Cambrensis - Wild, Untamed and Free.

Autumn Sun

You wept bitterly in the early autumn sun.
Golden tears turned from the sky in a
Glorious array of colour vibrant life
Littered away in a stray breeze.

Grieving the splendour
The majestic arch stands bereft.
Mourning the life once proud in the sun
now a desolate carpet of decay.

The last goodness leaches out into the
damp soil beneath as mists condense
in a waning sun. Come now
see what death has become.

Out of the warm blanket of leaves,
rising toward the empty canopy
which gave it life, hibernation breaks
with new growth in the midst of chaos.

One life gives legacy for the other
the warm sap rises and the last sweet song
of the leaf is not her autumn colours.
As winter despair gives way to hope that,
a new canopy will rise from the ashes of the last.

Empty Vase

With what shall I fill this vase?

Vacant without expectations

to be filled as others will this day.

A hedgerow flower, a sprig of

rosemary mourning the absence

no bouquet will relieve?

Fill it then to bursting, blooms and blossoms

which mask our sadness for a time

already wilting, dead from the moment

they were cut from the earth.

An empty vase echoes the empty tomb,

pierced heart of Mary's womb.

A beauty which only love can buy.

Space Between the Trees

I'll not see you, Callum, save for a glimpse

Of the shadows that you leave

In the spaces between trees

Or on mountains and hills

Riding swift and free.

And I'll hear your voice echo

As the wind through the valley

Unique in it's way to say what you mean

do what you say, No lying, half measures,

No hidden agendas.

You'll be there still somehow, in the caring

you showed, in your way, In friends

brought together in the forest lakes and rivers.

with a focussed attention and passion.

Freestyle, they call it, not skiing or biking, but life

With the right kit, or without - just out -

When the gaps between the trees closed on your life we were left in your wake.
More behind than before.

The way through the trees
which you found remains hidden.

So I'll not see you, Callum,
save for a glimpse
Of the shadows that you leave
In the space between the trees
on the mountains and hills
Riding swift and free.

Eternity

What is Eternity but every moment unending.
The quiet conversation where two souls kiss
in the silent yearning of their hearts.
A meeting of friends when, companion
means more than the bread we share.
When journeys continue in our mind long after
standing close sharing warmth
silently contemplating stars.

Laughing with those who
never thought they would laugh.
Caught in a moment on a mountain
as all fades to grey.

Walking through crowded fields
as if a dream unfolds alone
Carrying the brokenness of others
as if it were my own
Holding the tears that pierce our hearts
long after the sharp pain is dull
Dancing to the rhythm in the bones of my soul
a journey shared on a path without control of
eternity that began, begins, and brings us to the close.

What Is Gone

The shadows shine

Darkly behind all they were

An imprint of their lives upon our own

Outlines remain yet nothing inhabits the space

Memories on an ink pad never refreshed

Become background noise to the daily clamour

Threads all but gone yet woven still

Half remembered conversations drift

Waking dreams of lives entangled till

Fading echos draw away

Our past their's forever

What is gone

Is gone, no more.

Creation

In the half light
shade nor shadow
yet distinguished.

Expectations come
of a dawning; for all
in that moment to be
well before sleep has
properly passed. The

beauty of that fragile
garden now all but
out of reach save for
a glimpse of light
between trees in
muffled footsteps in the
stillness of the morning

A softening of breath gives
credence to all that exists

Chaos

Now the darkness,

watch and pray.

Prayer turns to sleep

to prayer to sleep again.

A moment away in another garden,

that this cup might pass,

might there yet be another way?

Knowing how reconciliation would come:

Piercing the night, betrayals, trampled underfoot.
Soldiers, torches, swords, clubs, accusations.

Flee away

Re-Creation

Beauty and fragility once

honoured in the garden

broken now. Anxious silence.

Anticipation closes in.

The stillness of daybreak;

sunset almost, a last glimpse of

reconciling light.

Now is the aftermath

of wood and stone;

Autumn Saint Autumn Sun

An autumn sun for an autumn saint
sits low and pale behind the mists of
the morning as a million lost causes
hang on to tree branches in a final
colourful prayer of disobedience.

A stray breeze releases them to the ground.

Is that a prayer I choose this day?
To be released. Or is it to stay for one
final warming of the sun before the
slow drift to rest?

Across the bridge to the north the last
of the mist shuffles away between trees
and rocks. Another offering off toward
the skies as our morning prayers take
flight. As we leave, the day began, the
mists have gone. Our cause as lost as
dear St. Jude. The last chance offering
of empty 'just-in-cases' to carry us on
to the whatever of tomorrow.

Morning Prayer

There is a sweetness to the air on
the hillside rising up through the mists
as the trees, cleansing, gently exhale.
Precious moments. The mountains
appear crisp in sharp focus, even in the
early sun. A thick fog, opaque, hangs low
reluctant to move on settled at the bottom
of the valley - under construction, perhaps.
It is I who need my weariness refreshed
recreating anew each day lightness,
easiness of step enabling me to carry the
brightness above, to join the trees giving life,
as wisps of cloud unfurl and tension drifts away.

The Cat

Returning cold and wet from a Saturday morning run despite rain jacket, hat and gloves I am greeted by The Cat sitting on the back porch, looking rather smug, out of the rain.

His greeting, a loud, extended and I suspect annoyed 'Meaow'.

I presume this to mean one of the following: Firstly, where is my breakfast? - usual answer: in your bowl as always.

Second: Would you mind changing the weather please?

He would if he could on to suggest that since I am the vicar and he the vicar's cat, surely he ought to get preferential treatment in the weather department and seeing as it is Saturday and everything and his real staff are due to visit at any moment would you please see to it that it is dry enough to venture out for a pee.

I spare him the theological reasoning as to why this is nonsense, ignore his protests and proceed indoors in search of dry clothing and some much needed coffee.

On my return to the kitchen however, The Cat's complaint seems to be repeated. His usual affectionate kitchen antics around my ankles are now more like a trip hazard. Clearly he is not to be satisfied with a fresh bowl of food.

Whilst the coffee is brewing, I scoop him up into his usual perch on my arm at which point the internal motor begins and a third possibility arises from his loud complaint.

He too is wet. I, now dry, am the perfect object on which he can dry himself.

This complete, he marches off indoors in search of a cushion or two, curls up in the distinct ball that only a cat can create metaphorically erecting a sign that says 'do not disturb'.

I am left, as usual, baffled by all this palaver and return in search of the coffee pot, not to mention of course, I'm now in need of a change of jumper.

Internally I note that as The Cat cannot change his jumper, his need really was greater than mine and as the door to the location of the favourite cushion was closed whilst I was out, his complaint - lodged in triplicate, seemed to have been upheld.

My rather wistful musings on the state of the weather whilst out on my run now seem to pale in comparison to The Cat's way of being - 'ask and you shall receive, ask loudly and the door shall be opened, complain a third time and your fur will be dried for you.'

In Memoriam - a Last Pair of Shoes

My grandfather always seemed to wear the same shoes. Not, of course, the same pair. Like all things they eventually needed replacing.

Each pair got demoted when the new ones arrived. Sunday shoes, well polished, lived by the front door.

Beneath them on the rack were the most recent pair of work shoes. From there they began the slow march of demotion into the kitchen to the back porch where at least two pairs of general garden, garage and DIY shoes lived.

Finally, the oldest were to be found out into the shed living in a box, a term I suspect to be quite literally true given their state. These were, as I recall, occasionally selected for digging potatoes.

Wanting to replace my comfortable dusty brown ankle boots, comfortable, easy on the feet. I began the search for another pair just the same as the previous two, like grandfather like grandson I thought.

Two pairs, both now letting water in at the bottom not even good for potato digging (and squeaking). The second-hand sources seem to have dried up.

And if I'm honest I don't really want a trail of discarded shoes. What I really would like is a pair that would last and be able to be repaired.

In need of some inspiration of where to look I thought of Lloyd, a friend and colleague whose sudden departure from this life has left its legacy.

When someone dies and the true sense of loss begins to dawn, hopefully too the legacy of the person who died begins to show through more strongly. Lloyd's legacy to me, so far, is a pair of shoes. Or, at least, the inspiration of how and where to look.

He was fastidious in his research from beloved cars to pairs of jeans the latter made in Wales to last - the Hiut Jeans no-wash club meant that in Lloyd's freezer amongst the frozen peas you would have found at least one pair of Jeans. Products designed to last or be repaired.

So with Lloyd's inspiration I began the search. It didn't take long to find the company in Machynlleth RED, Ruth Emily Davey, who by hand, makes shoes to fit your feet. They are made to last and be repairable.

This was not going to be a fast transaction of click and collect.

Arriving at RED in the town of Machynlleth I felt a rather nostalgic Dickensian wave of 'small boy outside toy shop' nose pressed to the window soaking up an image of the all too wonderful things that were within, but out of reach.

Entering that space, the world slowed, the colours more vivid somehow than the bright morning out of which I had just stepped.

With tea and gentle conversation we reflected and shared stories of loss. Mine of Lloyd whose inspiration had brought me here, and of Alan, Ruth's mentor who had died earlier in the year.

Feet were duly measured. Styles, colours, height of heel, fastenings were all discussed. Eyelets, leathers and linings chosen from those carefully displayed around me.

I'm too soon for the local leather, grown and tanned not three miles from the centre of the town. Perhaps I'll have to come again for a truly Welsh pair.

However, I break from what I've been wearing. The soft leather drab green boots have a flash of colour in the lining and will be ready in five weeks. In honour of this timescale I should take the bus to collect them, or perhaps the train. On reflection though it would have been faster to cycle.

Yet hurrying life onwards does us no favours. On a warm showery day at the end of June I returned to collect both the new handmade pair of boots and, because I just couldn't resist keeping them going for at least one more season, a repaired pair of the old dusty brown boots (no longer squeaking). It seems they too will have a new lease of life.

I'm offered the new boots wrapped within an elegant box. Ruth's smile that of creator, curator of a moment in which Christmas and birthday unwrappings are found wanting are reminders of gifts from children eager to see a parents' reaction to what they have made.

The unmistakable feet shaped shoes of RED contained. I always thought I had wide feet - I don't particularly. I have feet shaped feet and these shoes are made to match.

My hand knitted socks catch on the new suede lining. I'll need to unlace and lace these properly. I hear the age-old mandate ringing in my head.

Once within though, the soft leather cradles my feet. The close fit is quite unlike wearing shoes at all, more like a part of me through which I feel grounded, yet at the same time gently protected.

They are an expression of the wearer: drab green exterior, colour within.

I'll wear them with the top eyelet open and a little of the bright lining exposed.

'Will you wear them?' Ruth asks. Of course!

I leave the shop in new shoes with the old, repaired pair, tucked away in the box destined for potato digging and recycling in the shed.

Printed and bound by CPI Group (UK) Ltd, Croydon, CR0 4YY
14/10/2024
01773448-0002